HOLY LISTENING

with Breath, Body, and the Spirit

WHITNEY R. SIMPSON

UPPER
ROOM BOOKS®
NASHVILLE

Upper Room Books® website: books.upperroom.org

Upper Room®, Upper Room Books®, and design logos are trademarks owned by The Upper Room®, Nashville, Tennessee. All rights reserved.

Scripture quotations not otherwise marked are from the New Revised Standard Version Bible, copyright 1989 National Council of the Churches of Christ in the United States of America. Used by permission. All rights reserved.

Scripture quotations marked CEB are from the Common English Bible. Copyright © 2011 Common English Bible. Used by permission.

Yoga posture illustrations are taken from Sequence Wiz. Used by permission. www.sequencewiz.com

Cover design: Faceout Studio | faceoutstudio.com
Cover image: Stocksy
Interior design and typesetting: PerfecType | Nashville, TN

Library of Congress Cataloging-in-Publication Data

Names: Simpson, Whitney R., author.
Title: Holy listening with breath, body, and the spirit / Whitney R. Simpson.
Description: Nashville : Upper Room Books, 2017. | Includes index.
Identifiers: LCCN 2016029269| ISBN 9780835816311 (print) | ISBN 9780835816328
   (mobi) | ISBN 9780835816335 (epub)
Subjects: LCSH: Hatha yoga. | Mind and body—Religious aspects.
Classification: LCC RA781.7 .S558 2017 | DDC 613.7/046—dc23
LC record available at https://lccn.loc.gov/2016029269

Printed in the United States of America

For my family members, who have supported and encouraged this healing journey.
For each listener, caregiver, mentor, teacher, student, and friend along the path.
For you and your willingness to listen with the body God created.
For God's gift of peace.

The spirit of God has made me,
and the breath of the Almighty gives me life.
—Job 33:4

CONTENTS

SAFETY NOTICE

The information in this book is intended for educational purposes only. The advice shared is based on one individual's personal experiences and research. It is not intended to diagnose, prescribe, or treat any emotional, physical, or spiritual condition, illness, or injury. The author, publisher, and distributors of this book retain no liability or responsibility with respect to information shared in this book. If you are pregnant, nursing, or have health concerns, please contact your health-care provider prior to beginning this journey.

INTRODUCTION

The Lord God formed the human from the topsoil of the fertile land and blew life's breath into his nostrils. The human came to life.

—Genesis 2:7, CEB

God is the giver of life and breath. Miraculously, your breath flows in and out of your body, offering life. You live in the physical sense with your body and in the spiritual sense with your spirit; yet, no life exists—either in the body or spirit—without the starting point of the breath. While there are surely moments in this life that literally take your breath away—some good, some not so good—each breathtaking moment can only occur because of the moment when God first gave you breath. Since that first breath, each moment has shaped you, molded you, and made you into the person God created—one breath at a time.

I believe the Creator calls you to consider and embrace each moment of your life—and not simply the easy or happy ones. Both my body and spirit have sustained wounds. By listening to and reflecting on the pain my body and spirit have suffered, I begin a journey that will lead me toward healing and wholeness and a deeper relationship with God.

God created you as an amazing and complex human being. Science proves over and over that your body holds more wisdom than you can fathom. Your physical body also carries trauma and pain. No matter where you are on your healing journey, you are processing the traumas your body and spirit have experienced in the past.[1] As a Christian, you look to Jesus as your model for living. Jesus not only experiences many mountaintop moments but also encounters great physical trauma and pain. So what can Jesus' life teach you today about your body?

The gift of Jesus' incarnation is pivotal to the Christian faith, and it invites you to live out your belief with your whole self. As Flora Slosson Wuellner states, "Because our faith is rooted in the incarnation of Jesus, any form of spirituality we claim must also be incarnational, which by definition includes the wholeness of the person."[2] I believe the gift of the body (wounds and all) is the most intimate way to connect with God. A life with God invites you to be honest with yourself—to admit your weaknesses and tender spots. It also asks that you allow yourself to be shaped into the likeness of Christ in order not only to better yourself but also to better the world around you. This is the path of spiritual formation. M. Robert Mulholland Jr. defines Christian spiritual formation as "the process of being conformed to the image of Christ for the sake of others."[3] And so you must ask yourself, *Am I open to be being transformed? Am I willing to be transformed in these ways for the sake of the world? And if so, how do I begin?*

I often hear people say that focusing on listening to their own bodies, which requires slowing down and making space for reflection and change, feels selfish or uncomfortable. Though the spiritual formation journey begins within, it is far from selfish because it continues beyond the self to impact the lives of others. As for discomfort, honoring your body with time and space for God's healing touch is vital. Your body longs for this space on the journey of spiritual formation, and it is an important step toward healing and wholeness. Still, making space in your life for prayer and solitude—two disciplines upheld by many in Christian circles—may feel as if you are fighting against the societal norms of a noisy, fast-paced world. When you are unsure, look to the life of Jesus as an example.

In the Gospels, Jesus models the importance of prayer and solitude. (See Matthew 14:23; Mark 1:35; and Luke 5:16.) Do you long for time away with your Creator? Does it seem as if you can never escape the crowds of people in your life? Is your body calling out for you to slow down or start paying greater attention? Consider Jesus' actions in Matthew 14:23: "After he had dismissed the crowds, he went up the mountain by himself to pray." While climbing a mountain may be out of your comfort zone (or geographically impossible based on where you live), time with God—despite your location—can feel mountainous.

I encourage you to use this book as a guide on your journey toward healing, wholeness, and spiritual formation. Give yourself permission to slow down and listen to your body. Your journey will be enriched by quiet time spent away from the crowds and noise of life. Time apart with God is the balm your wounds need.

As you consider both your longings and wounds, you may be wondering if your past hurts have been prohibiting you from making the climb or departing from the crowd. In response, I simply offer Jesus as an example. After Jesus spends time away with God, he can then extend God's goodness to many. Spiritual formation starts with you and then impacts the world around you. Being shaped into the likeness of Christ for the benefit of yourself and others is a privilege.

After great physical trauma in my life, I had little choice but to begin listening more deeply to the wisdom of my body. As I began my healing process, I thirsted for more of a "with God" life. This desire eventually led me toward seminary course-work in the field of spiritual formation as well as yoga teacher trainings and certifica-tions. Over the course of this journey, I grew in knowledge and discovered many ideas worth embracing and sharing. In my years of searching, I never came to a healing and wholeness destination. Healing and wholeness don't come once you reach a certain age, once your pants fit, once you discover community, once your body does not ache, or even once you author a book about healing. Healing and wholeness provide a lifelong opportunity to journey with God.

God has already given you everything you need to live a whole life—no matter your hurts or wounds. Over the years, I told myself that if I were in good health, had a rewarding job, made good choices as a parent, spent time with people I cared about, and had the right tools for listening to God, I would finally discover God's peace. Instead, while I am grateful for rewarding and fruitful seasons of life, no latest and greatest item, season, skill, or technique will draw me nearer to God. Getting a good report from the doctor or being out of debt may offer comfort, but they will not fos-ter a relationship with God. By prioritizing time and space with God and learning the ways you best connect with your Creator, you may find you already have everything you need to listen for God.

While listening with your body (with the exception of your ears) may sound like an impossible concept, I encourage you to consider the miracle of your creation. God created your body and gave you breath to sustain your life. In the next forty days, I invite you to embrace the gift you have been given. Accepting the invitation does not mean you must have certain physical abilities or even a healthy relationship with your body. As you listen, may your ability to hear, see, experience, and appreciate God grow. Exploring the gift of your body—imperfections and all—will place you on a path toward healing and wholeness. No matter where you find yourself on this journey, God is with you.

The Gospel of John states the promise Jesus offers his disciples: " 'Peace be with you. As the Father has sent me, so I send you.' When he had said this, he breathed on them and said to them, 'Receive the Holy Spirit' " (20:21-22). Jesus breathes on them and gives the gift of the Holy Spirit. Earlier in the Gospel, Jesus offers his disciples the promise that God's Spirit will remain with them. (See John 14:26.) This promise extends to you today; the Holy Spirit is with you.

Holy listening is listening for God. I invite you to practice doing so with your breath, body, and spirit. Consider what could happen if you allowed yourself the space to slow down and embrace your whole self—breath, body, and spirit. How could it impact your journey of healing? My intention with this guide is not to answer that question but to make space for you to find your own answers. This guide will also tell some of my story—how I began the practice of holy listening with my own wounded, traumatized, imperfect, and magnificently created body.

Only you (and your Creator) are the expert when it comes to your body. What is God wanting you to discover? Flora Slosson Wuellner writes, "There are no easy, glib rules and answers. Our understanding and awareness of our bodily selves unfold slowly as we grow, learn, and mature within God's embrace."[4] My prayer for you is that you sense God's embrace as you listen with the gift of your body.

WHAT BRINGS YOU HERE?

One question I enjoy asking of others is, "What brings you here?" Pause and ask yourself, *Why am I holding this book? What does my body have to offer me on my spiritual formation journey? What do I long for on the journey of healing and wholeness? How are my breath, body, and spirit connected? Am I willing to slow down and listen to explore that connection with God? Am I open to the wisdom my body may share with me?*

While I was hesitant at first to understand or appreciate the deep connectedness among breath, body, and spirit, my life experiences have invited me over and over to pay attention to the wisdom from within. And I think "What brings you here?" is an important question to ask of anyone with whom I choose to journey in the spiritual life. For that reason, I would like to share my own story—a little of what brings me to this place.

In my early teenage years, I wanted to pursue a career as either a physical therapist or a youth pastor. While very different jobs, these two roles excited me, and I now recognize how each includes aspects of caring for body and spirit. I pursued neither as careers but instead completed a communications degree in college, which led to work in nonprofit organizations. That time was fruitful and introduced me to many great people and valuable causes. Yet, in ways I could never have imagined, my life later took a turn that led me away from a full-time career in the nonprofit world and led me closer to the roles I envisioned as a girl. God led me toward connecting breath, body, and spirit.

December 14, 2005, was my thirty-first birthday. Thirty seemed like a milestone, but I wasn't expecting much for thirty-one. I was looking forward to a quiet morning and a family celebration later in the day. What I experienced instead was beyond my imagination.

From Thanksgiving until my birthday that year, I had suffered a horrible case of asthmatic bronchitis that landed me in the hospital for over a week. So when I awoke in the early morning hours of December 14th not feeling well, I was not surprised as

I had not felt well in weeks. I was surprised, however, that the left side of my body was numb and tingly. I felt as if a ton of bricks were pushing down on my left side so forcefully I truly could not breathe. I also felt extraordinarily thirsty and confused.

With my husband sleeping soundly beside me and our almost two-year-old son in the room next door, I decided to get a glass of juice. I was certain that if I gave myself a few minutes, the feeling would soon pass. It did not. As I walked the short distance to the kitchen, my left foot oddly dragged the ground. I reached for the refrigerator door but could not make my left arm connect with the door handle. I vaguely remembered a connection between left arm pain and heart attacks and wondered if that was what I was feeling. But I wasn't only experiencing left arm pain; my left leg was also uncoordinated and weak. My symptoms made no sense to me. I was only able to move clumsily, as if the signals in my brain were not firing to tell my left hand or leg where or how to move. The only thing I knew to do in such a state was to Google my symptoms.

My inability to lift my left leg caused me to trip up the few steps as I walked to the computer, and I fell flat on my face on the carpet. Instead of feeling alarmed in that moment, I was simply confused. Once I settled in front of the computer, my fingers hit the keyboard, searching things like "left-side weakness." But my search terms looked something like this: "ldjz-wizr qxdkntxx." I suddenly realized my right hand was typing the correct keys while my left hand was randomly hitting keys on the keyboard. I was too exhausted to figure out what was happening, so I moved away from the computer and fell asleep on the couch. After a brief nap, I awoke with a gnawing feeling that my symptoms were likely not side effects of my previous illness but a serious problem. The numbness was not going away, and I knew something was wrong.

I finally woke my husband to explain the odd feeling on my left side. Wide-eyed and alert, he urged me to call my doctor. He wanted to drive me immediately to the emergency room, but I insisted on taking a shower and eating breakfast first. Though seemingly ridiculous actions, my previous hospital experience told me that I might not get to take a shower or eat real food for a few days.

At the hospital, the ER nurses rushed me into a room. Seated in front of an emergency physician, I tried to explain away my symptoms. I told him that they were merely a weird reaction or side effect due to the medication I had taken for my lungs and bronchitis. The physician kindly listened to my reasoning but explained that my theory was highly unlikely—if not impossible. He suggested that we talk further after an MRI.

An MRI scanner is a long, hollow tube surrounded by a giant magnet, and one has to lie still during the procedure. This was my first such experience—definitely not my last—and after being rushed into a room at the ER and finally feeling the weight of what could be wrong with me, I was suddenly more nervous than ever. The MRI scanned my head and neck for answers to the odd sensation in my left side. It was loud; it was cold; it was hollow. I felt alone.

During my MRI, I unexpectedly experienced the gift of God's peace. I began repeating four words over and over: *Jesus, give me peace*. In that moment, they were the only words I could think of, and they kept me calm. They became my breath prayer, inhaling and exhaling the words. The scan lasted over an hour, and I simply repeated in my head with each breath, *Jesus, give me peace*. God, present in the Trinity through Father, Son, and Holy Spirit, overwhelmed me on my birthday with this gift of peace.

I had no idea that day where the words came from. I simply knew they centered and grounded me. The prayer gave me peace and hope. Only years later, as I began writing this book, did the impetus for that prayer surface. As I flipped through stacks of old journals and books for glimpses into my own past, I recalled that four years prior to whispering my prayer in the MRI, I had completed a small-group study called *Companions in Christ*. Just a few pages were marked or highlighted in my copy of the book. As I turned to the page introducing breath prayer, I saw a giant asterisk and my own handwritten prayer, asking God to give me peace. Four years before I needed God's gift of peace in an intimate and desperate way, God planted this prayer in my heart.

The MRI found a mass, which I was told was between the size of a golf ball and tennis ball, at the base of my brain. This was not the news I expected to hear and certainly not what I hoped to receive on my birthday. The discovery was of even greater concern given a malignant melanoma that doctors had found when I was twenty-three. Melanoma is a form of skin cancer that can prove deadly if not treated or removed. My doctors knew of my cancer history and were prepared for the fact that it had returned. Soon I began experiencing seizures, which only caused more confusion regarding my diagnosis and overwhelmed my caregivers. I was sent by ambulance to a larger hospital, one more equipped to manage my situation, that December day. On the bumpy, cold ride, I continued to repeat my prayer: *Jesus, give me peace*. In the back of my mind, I asked myself, *How is it possible to be at peace in my spirit yet overwhelmed, exhausted, and confused in my body?* I would explore this question later as I began to understand how my body and spirit were deeply connected and why that connection mattered. Indeed, I learned later that the connection of the whole self is key to the healing journey.

The next forty-eight hours offered a glimpse of my new reality: being unable to use utensils to eat a simple hospital meal, creating a living will, juggling a young child between family members, and seeing the concerned faces of those who cared deeply for me. After brain scans, brain mapping, and meeting with multiple physicians, a plan was made for a craniotomy (brain surgery) to remove the mass at the base of my brain. This mass was causing my weakness, lack of coordination, and confusion. I slept through a portion of this story as my family, clergy, friends, and strangers prayed for my procedure.

After the surgery, my family received shockingly good news while I remained in recovery. The doctors had found no cancer, no tumor, no mass. The suspicious area, which had shown up on every scan, had dissipated and only minor surgery was needed. Simply put, my brain was tumor-free, and the surgeons and specialists, though pleased with my physical well-being, could offer no explanation for the mass's disappearance. I spent my days recovering in the ICU while doctors tried to determine what had happened to me. The pressure on my brain had caused me to have a stroke, but the doctors did not understand what had caused the original mass or how it disappeared. I was a stroke survivor, the cause of which was inconclusive, and the word *miracle* was whispered over me more than once.

After my surgery and recovery, I was moved to a facility where I could work on regaining my strength. My birthday had passed, and Christmas was approaching. I entered my new room in a wheelchair, swollen and puffy from medicine and sore and exhausted from days in bed. With my newly shaved head, I smiled and proudly greeted my neighbors. They were also mostly bald but not from brain surgery; I was by far the youngest resident in my rehabilitation facility. Most of my neighbors were old enough to be my grandparents, and they were kind and encouraging. I had so much work to do that I felt I may be their age by the time I left, but God had other plans.

I arrived at the rehab center just in time for my family to celebrate Christmas. My almost two-year-old son was thrilled to see me, and we sat on the floor playing with the occupational therapy team's building blocks. We did not open gifts. Our day was peaceful and uneventful. At my request—mainly because I was overwhelmed by any movement or noise—we simply spent quiet time together as a family that day. Once Christmas passed, however, I began to make steady progress with physical, speech, and occupational therapists. The overachiever in me kicked in, and I only stayed in the facility for a week of intense sessions. The doctors worked with me in an around-the-clock effort to encourage my left arm and leg to function fully, to clarify my speech, and to teach me to shower and dress myself, although at a new, slower pace. I continued to repeat my prayer: "Jesus, give me peace."

The new year brought the good news that I could go home. Still, I was only at the beginning of my healing journey. No longer in a wheelchair, I made my way to the couch in my home with a new cane and gazed at the Christmas tree. I had not yet been able to fully enjoy it; we had only put it up two days before my stroke. It was covered in a lifetime collection of Nativity ornaments my parents had given me for my birthday every year since 1974. Tears overwhelmed me that day in the shadow of the nativity scenes and lights. They were tears of relief, sadness, exhaustion, hope, thanksgiving, joy, and peace. I experienced God's peace at the foot of the tree—a tree that celebrated Christ's birth and my own. What a relief to be home again. That particular birthday offered me more than an ornament; instead, I received the gift of peace.

God continues to guide my journey along the road of healing and wholeness. And this journey includes an invitation to listen with my body and honor it as a gift from God. I am human and make mistakes often, but I have been given a gift that grounds me and humbles me every day: peace. This gift allows me to value and honor my body, including its imperfections. This gift also creates in me a longing to listen for God with each breath I take and to invite you to do the same.

In scripture, as with my story, the word *peace* is often considered a gift. It is interpreted with various meanings including "wholeness" and "well-being." Choose to explore God's gift of peace today. A crisis is not required to learn how to listen for God's activity in and around you, to use your breath and body, and to recognize God's Spirit dwelling in you. This book will guide you in engaging your whole self as you slow down to listen for God and explore the gift of God's peace.

HOLY LISTENING

In telling my story, I fast-forwarded through years of doctor's visits, follow-up scans, inconclusive results of the cause of stroke, chronic pain, physical therapy, counseling, spiritual direction, yoga, holistic healing, and general recovery time. Every ounce of my being wanted to rush through this season of recovery, but my body had a new, slow pace. I had many opportunities to practice listening with my body as I explored the gift of God's peace.

During my time of recovery from my stroke and brain surgery, listening for God eventually became more natural. Early on, I experienced long stretches of loneliness and quiet. Some days, the only other voice in my home was Oprah Winfrey's as I walked laps around the couch to fulfill my physical therapist's exercise assignments.

One of the biggest struggles I experienced during my recovery was losing the ability to multitask. One evening as my family was sitting down to enjoy a casserole dropped off by a friend from church, I tried to explain to my husband an episode of *Oprah* while I dished out my dinner at the same time. I couldn't do it. My coordination was comparable to that of our two-year-old. I couldn't tell the story and put food on my plate at the same time. I could stop talking and scoop the casserole, or I could talk without scooping the casserole. It was a simple task—preparing a plate—and was something I had done without a thought before my stroke. Yet my body and brain weren't able to work together in that way. I collapsed onto the floor and cried tears of frustration. *Will I ever be able to do more than one thing at a time?* I wondered. *Why am I being limited in this way?* I had no choice but to listen to my body and focus on one task at a time as I cried out to God.

Yet even this struggle offered treasures in the long run. While I have improved greatly in my ability to multitask, I now recognize and understand that my limitation has served me well in certain ways. My inability to function at a level to which I was previously accustomed—a level our world tells us is relatively healthy—forced me into a listening space with God, one I never could have envisioned for myself. I began to understand deep listening in a brand-new way, and the new pace of my body was largely to thank for the opportunity. God was knitting my experiences together with my breath and body and drawing me nearer to God's Spirit within.

This time of recovery also brought moments of clarity when God nudged me to become a formal student again. God led me to pursue seminary coursework and yoga teacher trainings in ways that would not have been possible had I still been able to plow through life with abandon and full capabilities. God made space in my life, and I began to learn to listen in a new, deeper way. I now companion others as they listen for God's activity using the tools of both spiritual direction and yoga.

Traditionally, spiritual direction takes place between an individual directee and a trained spiritual director. Formal spiritual direction may also occur in a group format with a spiritual director and multiple directees. Though this book will guide you as you learn to listen with your body, it cannot be a substitute for a listening companion on your journey. You may wish to contact a spiritual director, spiritual friend, counselor, or other trusted person to accompany you as you engage your body and spirit. While a personal companion or guide may allow for a broader experience, remember that you are the only one who has the ability to listen with your body. Therefore, this devotional invites you into a personal time of holy listening and reflection with your Creator God.

The ancient practice of spiritual direction offers time for holy listening without expectations or assumptions. Spiritual directors nudge their directees to ask questions rather than offering them answers. A directee is encouraged to listen for God's answers. A spiritual director helps a directee distinguish between God's voice and other competing voices—sometimes his or her own, sometimes others' voices.[1] If you have never met with a spiritual director, I encourage you to consider learning more about the practice. In her book, *Holy Listening: The Art of Spiritual Direction,* Margaret Guenther demystifies the role of a spiritual director. She describes the calling of a spiritual director as a midwife for the soul—a description that captures how a spiritual director longs to safely companion others.[2] As a spiritual director, I hope this book guides you in holy listening as you connect with your breath, body, and spirit through the daily themes and exercises. May the tools included in the book companion you and invite you to listen for God's activity in your life.

God gifted you with a body. On this particular journey of practicing holy listening, you will use your entire being—mind, muscles, senses, imagination, and breath—in listening for God's activity in and around you. You may find that you complete this book in forty days and then return to a particular day's practice. You may journey with one day's practice for an entire week—or even longer. Though this guide invites you into a period of personal awareness and individual reflection, you may choose to work through the book with others in a small group. If you engage with the book as part of a group, remember that no two members' journeys will be the same. Work with fellow group members to create a safe space for discussion, knowing that one person's experience may be different than your own. To this end, I have included some helpful tips at the back of the book for small groups.

As you begin to listen more deeply with breath, body, and spirit, take time to notice the holy amidst both the ordinary and the extraordinary, the loud and the quiet. Prepare to listen for God's activity with all your being and to experience God's peace.

FORTY DAYS

This devotional guide consists of forty themed invitations. I designed each invitation to foster quiet space for your breath, body, and spirit. Each invitation consists of the following activities:

- scripture reading with *lectio divina*
- two yoga postures
- a breath prayer
- an aromatherapy scent using essential oils
- reflection questions for journaling or other creative expression

If some of these listening tools are new or unfamiliar to you, consider trying them anyway. You may choose to engage in each daily activity, or you may only work with a few. There is no correct or incorrect way to use this book as you practice holy listening. The activities for any given day are designed to be completed in thirty minutes to one hour, but you can spend as much time on a theme as you are able.

The number of days selected for this journey—forty—holds much significance. That number is often associated with times of testing and clarity in scripture. (See Genesis 7:12; Exodus 24:18; Matthew 4:2; and Acts 7:30.) The book's forty-day format lends itself to be used during Lent but could be used during Advent as well. You may follow the themes in order, or you may skip around, selecting a theme that speaks to you on a particular day. I thoughtfully chose each scripture passage, posture, prayer, scent, and reflection question based on research and experience for exploring the day's theme. (See page 129 for additional details on how each theme was chosen.) You may encounter themes that make you uncomfortable, but I hope you won't avoid those that seem challenging. Your body can teach you when you venture outside your comfort zone. If you feel called to focus on a day's theme for an extended period of time, give yourself the permission to do so. Revisit themes you have already practiced as needed. Ultimately, you will choose how you journey with and use this book.

This book was inspired by my own journey, but I created it for you—no matter where you find yourself on your journey toward healing and wholeness. I encourage you to offer yourself grace instead of allowing perfectionism to cast a shadow on this opportunity for listening. If you simply breathe and reflect, you have listened with your body. With that in mind, the next section offers an overview of each listening tool.

THE ANCIENT TOOLS

Each day's invitation focuses on a theme, and you will use the following tools to explore that theme: *lectio divina*, yoga, breath prayer, and aromatherapy. Along with these ancient tools, you may find journaling and creating a sacred space to be helpful in your healing journey.

Lectio Divina

The words *lectio divina* are Latin for "holy reading." This ancient prayer practice includes the following steps: *lectio* ("to read"), *meditatio* ("to reflect"), *oratio* ("to respond"), and *contemplatio* ("to rest"). *Lectio divina* allows you to listen for God's activity using scripture and to connect to God through the ancient Word while delving into a particular passage. The practice of *lectio divina* focuses on formational reading of scripture as opposed to informational reading.[1] Formational reading invites the text to shape you while informational reading invites you to understand the text.[2] Though both types of reading can be useful on a spiritual journey, the art of *lectio divina* allows you to interact with God's Word through meditating on a passage and listening for God's leading. My personal journey has been shaped by spending time in the Word using *lectio divina*. Through this practice, I have realized how scripture can speak to my life regardless of what I am facing. *Lectio divina* has allowed me to see and hear God in new ways.

If you are new to the practice of *lectio divina*, I have included a brief overview and instructions. Feel free to refer to these instructions until this style of holy reading and meditating on God's Word becomes natural to you. Though I have included each theme's scripture passage in its entirety, you may wish to read the passage in your own Bible or in a different Bible translation. You may also consider reading the scripture passages aloud or using an audio Bible or a Bible app that reads to you. I encourage you to explore various ways of interacting with God's Word as you practice *lectio divina*.

How to Practice Lectio Divina

Prepare yourself for this practice by inviting God to speak to you through a particular scripture passage as you enjoy being in God's presence.

1. **Lectio/Read.** Read or listen to the designated passage once slowly.
2. **Meditatio/Reflect.** Read or listen to the passage again. Consider a word, phrase, or image from the passage that draws your attention. What stands out to you? What do you hear, see, or sense? Reflect on how this word, image, or phrase speaks to you today. Consider repeating your word or phrase silently to yourself.
3. **Oratio/Respond.** Read or listen to the passage again. Respond to what you hear in God's Word and how it makes you feel. Is there an invitation for you—for your breath, body, or spirit—in the scripture passage today? Tell God what you heard or sensed.
4. **Contemplatio/Rest.** Rest in what you have heard. Receive any clarity, stillness, insight, or imagery that comes to your mind. Give God thanks for this time, and rest in the Word of God.

Yoga

Yoga is a practice that brings together mind, body, and spirit. With your intention set on God, yoga becomes a holy practice. As a Christian, my yoga practice and training combines the intention of focusing on God with the physical practice of yoga. For me, the mindfulness aspect of yoga is a spiritual discipline. When practiced as a spiritual discipline, yoga has the ability to transform your body and your spirit. In the book *Holy Yoga: Exercise for the Christian Body and Soul*, Brooke Boon writes, "While yoga cannot be considered a 'classical' spiritual discipline, it nevertheless has the same goal and can have similar effects as other disciplines, provided it is practiced with the right intent. It can take us into the depths of a relationship with Christ."[3] After over a decade of practicing yoga, I have found it to be an embodied prayer experience and a discipline that continues to yoke me to my Creator.

Yoga can spiritually transform you as you move with the intention of connecting with God. Stretching and breathing exercises can help you be less distracted during prayer and meditation, and they allow you to listen more deeply. Yoga as a spiritual discipline is less about exercise and more about giving your body and spirit the space to listen for and receive God's word.

Each daily theme includes two yoga postures for your exploration: a pose and a counterpose. A counterpose simply moves your body in the opposite direction of the designated pose or returns your body to a neutral position. I selected the two poses as a way for you to practice yoga in a short and safe sequence. Since some poses are used more than once, I hope that you will become more familiar with them as you revisit them. If you do not practice yoga or are not familiar with the postures, I've included written instructions for each pose in the appendix. Be aware that some poses should be practiced on both the left and right side of your body. You may choose to complete each day's practice in a seated meditation position in a chair or on the floor instead of the yoga poses provided. Chair modification options for selected poses are also available in the appendix. I hope that this guide will be accessible to all, regardless of physical capability.

Even if you have practiced yoga before, the postures used in this book may not be familiar to you. Yoga poses are passed from teacher to student and may be modified, described in a different way, or have a different name than how you learned them. The poses used in this book are indexed in the appendix using the English name and the traditional Sanskrit name. While the original Sanskrit is included in the appendix for reference and your own research, it is not necessary to understand Sanskrit to incorporate the postures into your practice.

Practicing yoga as a spiritual discipline requires much more than simply putting your body in different physical positions. In fact, focusing on your posture and breathing is a good place to start for beginners. Consider the poses in this book an invitation to discover those revelations God longs to reveal to you through your physical body. And, yes, you can still participate on this journey even if you are not a yoga practitioner! I was far from comfortable on a yoga mat when I began intentionally listening for God's activity in and around me.

Though I had attended a few yoga classes before my stroke, my journey with yoga began when my doctor prescribed it for chronic pain during my recovery. Even after receiving a doctor's recommendation, I was unsure it would help. At my first private yoga session, I refused to remove my shoes because I feared standing barefoot due to the pain I felt in my feet without my shoes as support. My patient and gracious teacher honored my request, and we practiced that first day with my shoes on. My point is this: Start where you are, and be open to the fact that God longs to meet you there.

Before practicing any yoga poses, I recommend warming up with gentle stretching. I have included a warm-up sequence with various stretches on pages 116–17.

During your warm-up and yoga practice, concentrate on your breathing so as not to hold your breath. Many techniques for breathing can be used in yoga. For now, simply focus on inhaling and exhaling through your nose in a slow and steady rhythm. I encourage you to hold each pose for five, ten, or fifteen breaths before moving to the counterpose. As you become more experienced in your yoga practice, your breaths may deepen and the amount of time you hold the postures may increase. Many yoga teachers believe that practicing yoga and breath work every day for short periods of time is as beneficial (if not more so) than practicing less regularly but for longer periods of time.

While you have all you need to begin practicing yoga with your own physical body and breath, you may wish to use props such as a yoga mat. My yoga mat eventually became a place that not only relieved my chronic pain but also allowed me to spend time with God. Additional props you may find helpful include a yoga blanket, block, and strap, all of which can be found at most retail stores or online. You may also discover simple items around your home to be useful in your practice. A towel can serve as a mat in a pinch, and a neck-tie can become a yoga strap. Where you practice is less important than actually practicing; however, a hard-surfaced floor space with accessibility to a wall or chair will offer more stability for your standing and balancing positions. No special clothes are needed, but you will want to dress comfortably, allowing for freedom of movement. And if you are willing and able, remove your shoes and socks to connect with the ground and prevent slipping.

As time allows, I encourage you to close your practice with the final resting pose of relaxation. (See page 128.) Upon completion of all forty themes, consider connecting the various postures you have explored to create your own longer yoga sequence, beginning with a warm-up, moving to postures, and ending with extended relaxation. Experienced yoga practitioners may find renewal and inspiration in their physical practice by incorporating the additional prompts for listening or creating a more advanced yoga sequence based on the daily pose and counterpose.

I hope this book will help you become comfortable with exploring yoga as a spiritual discipline. The following books offer further reading on using yoga in your Christian spiritual formation: *Holy Yoga: Exercise for the Christian Body and Soul* by Brooke Boon (FaithWords, 2007), *An Invitation to Christian Yoga* by Nancy Roth (Cowly Publications, 2001), and *Prayer of Heart & Body: Meditation and Yoga as Christian Spiritual Practice* by Thomas Ryan (Paulist Press, 1995).

This guide is designed to be beginner-friendly yet also challenging for experienced yoga practitioners. Some of the postures included in this book are advanced postures. If you are new to yoga, enjoy exploring both the simple and the challenging postures. Do what you can with the more difficult postures, and remind yourself to breathe. Be safe, always listening to your body's warning signs. For example, physical pain can alert you to modify or select another posture. This book is no substitute for in-person alignment and yoga instruction. If you long to expand your yoga practice, seek out an experienced and qualified instructor to companion you.

Breath Prayer

Every breath you take serves as a reminder of God's gift of life and the Spirit within. The Hebrew word *ruach* is used interchangeably in scripture for both breath and spirit, as is the Greek word *pneuma*. A breath prayer is a simple, intimate, and repetitive prayer that can be repeated during each inhalation and exhalation, drawing you nearer to the Spirit of God.[4] This contemplative practice links prayer to the rhythm of your own breath. The breath prayer from my birthday—*Jesus, give me peace*—became a powerful and constant reminder that God was with me on my healing journey. As you focus on each breath as a gift from God, your prayer becomes a living meditation too, an opportunity to "pray continually" (1 Thess. 5:17, CEB). A breath prayer involves two steps: breathing in and breathing out. When you breathe in, call on a biblical name or image of God. When you breathe out, express the longings of your heart or a God-given desire. Don't worry about where the words fall in your breathing pattern. Calling out to God with words may soon become as rhythmic as breathing.

Each daily theme includes a breath prayer. I encourage you to make these prayers personal over time. Use the written prayers as you become comfortable with breath prayer, then consider creating your own. Repeat your prayer so often that it becomes part of you and can easily be carried with you. If you need a reminder throughout the day, write your breath prayer on an index card and carry it with you.

While practicing the yoga postures and breath prayers in this book, explore the fullness of your breath by accessing the depths of your diaphragm. To practice diaphragmatic breathing (also called "belly breathing), sit tall in a chair, or, if this style of breathing is new to you, you may wish to lie on your back and place one hand on your belly and one on your chest. Take a few conscious breaths, inhaling and exhaling through your nose, and notice the pause in between each breath. Breathe deeply into your diaphragm and notice as your belly expands. Exhale and notice your abdomen contract. Consider the rise and fall of your belly as you breathe while the hand on your chest remains relatively still. Consider continuing your deep breathing as you incorporate your breath prayer for five or more minutes. I encourage you to practice deep breathing and breath prayer not only in your quiet prayer time but also during other moments throughout your day. Each breath is an opportunity to draw nearer to God.

Aromatherapy

Aromatherapy is the science and art of using extracts from plants to benefit the body, mind, and spirit. Essential oils use the earth's natural resources by incorporating various parts of a plant, including the bark, leaves, flowers, stems, or roots. Modern essential oils are created through processes such as steam distillation and expression. Oils mentioned in scripture were used in a variety of ways—anointing, healing, offerings, and burial. (See Exodus 29:7; Leviticus 2:15-16; Proverbs 7:17; Mark 16:1; John 12:3; John 19:39-40; and James 5:14.) Many biblical accounts point to an appreciation for and practical use of both aromatherapy and oils in ancient times. Consider, for example, the well-known first gifts to Jesus of frankincense and myrrh. Modern essential oils allow you to appreciate as well as experience the physical, spiritual, and emotional benefits of ancient aromatherapy.

In the book *Awaken to Healing Fragrance: The Power of Essential Oil Therapy*, Elizabeth Anne Jones explains the chemistry and complexity of essential oils. She writes, "Mind-body health is achieved when our thoughts, our emotions, and our physical bodies are in harmony, inspired by our inner spirit. Essential oils that work simultaneously on all levels are the perfect instruments to bring this about. They are the gifts from God in the plant world that magnetize us toward this optimum state of balance."[5]

While recovering from my stroke, I discovered my own state of balance as I began using essential oils in my home. I would diffuse rosemary and lemon for an inviting scent that lifted my spirits and kept my house smelling fresh. I used essential oils in this way for years before I recognized the healing benefits these oils were offering my body and spirit—much more than a freshened sacred space. While emotional and spiritual use has been my primary experience with oils, my family uses calming oils at night to sleep well and breathe more easily. I also use oils to boost my immunity and fight germs. My own journey with essential oils has confirmed that the benefits of their use are much greater than simply smelling like the great outdoors or, in some cases, a spice cabinet. I have a deep appreciation for the ancient practice of aromatherapy and consider essential oils a gift from God's creation that offer balance to my life.

Essential oils may be used in a variety of ways. For the purpose of simplicity, I have only suggested you use oils aromatically—by inhaling them through the nose.

Simply inhale the scent of the suggested oil from the bottle. Or place a small amount of the essential oil on a cotton ball, cup it in your hands, and inhale the scent. If you have a diffuser in your home, you may choose to diffuse the designated oil during your time of prayer and listening.

Upon inhalation, the oil passes through your lungs and send signals to your brain. Allow each scent to speak to your soul as you practice holy listening. Aromatherapy is a wonderful tool for drawing you nearer to God in spite of the busy-ness of your day. Let essential oils and aromatherapy remind you of God in times of prayer and during your daily routine.

While you may not own any or all of the essential oils included in this book, allow them to serve as a reference as you consider growing your own collection. If you are not interested in investing in an essential oil collection, consider deeply inhaling the next time you cut a lemon. The scent of freshly cut citrus allows you to experience the gift of your sense of smell. If you do wish to purchase your own essential oils, use caution and wisdom. Due to the popularity and increased use of essential oils today, they are widely available. In the United States, the essential oil market is not regulated by a government agency. I suggest researching the company you purchase from and noting its responsibility in harvesting oils, in providing third-party testing, in honoring and encouraging high safety precautions, and in protecting the integrity of indigenous plants. Connect with an aromatherapist if you have further questions. Also, remember that essential oils are very concentrated so a little oil goes a long way. Use these forty days to breathe deeply and discover the gift of aromatherapy.

Essential oils are not necessary for engaging with this resource. Even if you only have one essential oil, consider using it in your time of prayer and listening. Remember, you can also discover scents in your kitchen or garden. This content is meant for educational purposes only. The information regarding the aromatic use of essential oils is in no way intended to diagnose or treat emotional, spiritual, or physical conditions, illnesses, or injuries. If you are pregnant, nursing, or have health concerns, including sensitivities or allergies, find a certified or clinical aromatherapist or medical practitioner who is qualified to offer guidance. Some essential oils can be dangerous if not handled properly or are not safe for pregnant women or children. When used wisely, safely, and sparingly, essential oils can be a great tool for the spiritual journey.

Journaling

Journaling has been an important part of my healing journey and was encouraged by both my counselor and spiritual director after my stroke. The physical act of writing words by hand onto paper allowed an awareness of feelings I did not even recognize. Researchers have studied the benefits of journaling, and they continue to suggest that self-expression through journaling is a great resource for the healing process.[6]

I invite you to write and reflect during each of the forty days you use this book. The reflection questions at the end of each day's theme serve to help you discover your own longings. After you have listened with your body, read the questions and consider your responses. Do parts of your physical body tighten? Does your heart or stomach offer feedback? Does your breathing change? What are you feeling or sensing—physically or emotionally? Journaling is a tool for more than your mind. Allow your body and spirit to also take part while journaling any thoughts, feelings, or responses you had during your time of holy listening.

You may wish to journal in a notebook as I did. While I recognize the physical act of putting words to paper was important and formational for my own journey, I understand that not everyone savors that process. If you prefer recording your thoughts electronically, consider that as an option. While I have tried both handwritten and typed journaling, I find that I am more honest with myself in handwritten reflection rather than typed. When I'm typing, I tend to edit myself.

Regardless of your method, I suggest that you keep a written response to the themes in this book—you may even consider writing in the margins. If journaling is not something you have done before, give it a try for these forty days. You may also choose a different type of creative expression such as art, music, or poetry. Use your imagination and try not to limit yourself as you process and explore how God is speaking to you. Make time and space to reflect and respond through whatever means work best for you. Your journaling and reflection time invites you to rest in what you may have heard or experienced. Your journal may become a tool you return to for insight and wisdom.

Sacred Space

Finding a sacred space to listen with your body needn't be complicated. While many think only formal places of worship can be sacred spaces, discovering your own personal sacred space for times of quiet reflection can be truly beneficial. You may already have a sacred space in your home or in nature where you meet with God. If not, I encourage you to seek or create one with intention and discernment before you begin working through this book.

Preparing your sacred space can be as simple or as intricate as you want. Include a candle, a religious icon, a cross, or any other symbol of your faith journey in your sacred space, along with any other supplies you need to participate in the daily activities—a journal, writing utensil, yoga mat (and props if needed), and essential oil. The only mandatory requirement for your sacred space is you—your breath, body, and spirit. Do your best to find a quiet place with as few distractions as possible. This will encourage the act of listening with your body. If escaping the noise of life is impossible due to roommates, children, a spouse, or other factors, consider wearing headphones and listening to quiet music. Discover creative ways to prioritize your time apart with God. Keeping your sacred space in a consistent location will make transitioning into your time of listening and reflecting easier.

Spiritual formation is for everyone; how you embrace the process is up to you. Henri Nouwen writes, "A spiritual life cannot be formed without discipline, practice, and accountability."[7] Discipline, practice, and accountability may be the aspects of my spiritual journey with which I struggle the most. Having a sacred space helps with this struggle. Discipline is key to the spiritual life, and a sacred space helps me consistently practice times of quiet listening with God. If possible, only use your sacred space for time with God. In other words, your sacred space shouldn't be where you pay bills or work.

The spiritual life is not formed accidentally; it takes effort and desire. Discovering a consistent time of day that works best for you may also help your time of holy listening to become a practiced ritual. Listening to your body may become a habit you guard and protect for the health of your emotional and spiritual life. I have sacred space set aside in my home, and I've stashed tools for prayer—a Bible, devotional book, prayer beads—in various corners of the house and car. They remind me to prioritize my listening time with God. And while this journey is one you can ultimately take anywhere, you will find that entering a dedicated sacred space at a designated time will soon feel like a homecoming.

THE INVITATION

When I'm preparing for a time of prayer, I often list in my head or on paper things I want to ask of God. Prayer lists remind me of my own longings and help me communicate my desires to God. Holy listening turns this type of prayer on its head. Instead of being concerned with what I will say to God, I can use the tools in this book to listen to what God may be saying to me through my breath, body, and spirit. Holy listening may come easy for you, or it may not. But this practice needn't be intimidating, overwhelming, or hard. Set aside your expectations and trust the still small voice within as you listen for God. May Flora Slosson Wuellner's words on prayer embolden you: "Yes, prayer *is* easier than we thought. Prayer was always meant to be part of our everyday lives, part of our bodies, part of all our actions."[1] Embrace this invitation to use your breath, body, and spirit to listen to God.

In scripture, the word *selah* concludes many psalms. While theologians do not know the exact definition of the word, some understand it as an invitation to pause. Each theme in this book is a *selah*. I don't know what you will discover, but I encourage you to pause and consider how God is speaking to you through your body. Delight in the process, and open yourself to the possibility of physical, spiritual, and emotional transformation.

REFLECTION QUESTIONS
BEFORE YOU BEGIN

- When do you experience silence in your life? How do you embrace those times of quiet? How are your breath, body, and spirit engaged in those times?
- Is it easy or hard for you to find stillness and silence in your life? In what ways have you sought stillness and silence in your breath, body, and spirit?
- Does prayer come naturally for you? If so, what is your current prayer practice? If not, reflect on your feelings toward prayer. Does the concept of prayer intimidate you? Do you struggle to listen for God?
- How would your relationship with God grow and change if you spent more time listening or in silence?
- If your life were free of noise and distraction, what would God want to say to you?
- How can you rid yourself of some of the noise or distractions in your life and spend time listening to God? How can creating a sacred space allow you to enter times of quiet listening and prayer?
- Who companions you on your spiritual journey or holds you accountable? Who can support you in this season of holy listening—trusted spiritual friends, peers, a spiritual director, a pastor, a counselor, or a mentor?
- How can caring for your body allow you to care for your spirit?
- How will you make space for holy listening in your life?

BE

Lectio Divina

Be still before the LORD,
and wait for him.

—Psalm 37:7, CEB

Pose

Legs-up-the-Wall

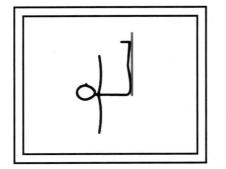

Counterpose

Corpse

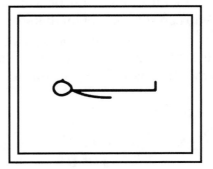

Breath Prayer

Inhale: Waiting for you, Lord,
Exhale: I will listen and be still.

Aromatherapy

Spruce

Reflect

What physical parts of you struggle to find stillness? In what areas of your life may God be asking you to embrace stillness? What part of you best embraces stillness—breath, body, or spirit? How can you embrace the person God has made you to be?

———

ACCEPT

Lectio Divina

You are the one who created my innermost parts;
   you knit me together while I was still in my mother's womb.
—Psalm 139:13, CEB

Pose	Counterpose
Camel	Child's Pose

Breath Prayer

Inhale: Lord, may I accept myself
Exhale: the way you created me.

Aromatherapy

Lime

Reflect

Considering how God knows your innermost parts, how can you accept yourself as God created you? Pray for the parts of yourself that you struggle to accept. Ask God today to show you how God sees and accepts you.

———

COMMIT

Lectio Divina

Now may you be committed to the Lᴏʀᴅ our God with all your heart by following his laws and observing his commands, just as you are doing right now.
—1 Kings 8:61, ᴄᴇʙ

Pose
Gate

Counterpose
Child's Pose

Breath Prayer

Inhale: Adonai,
Exhale: I am yours.

Aromatherapy

Cilantro

Reflect

How you spend your time, resources, and energy often shows what you value. To whom or what are you committed? Do you feel frustration, resistance, tightness, or a negative emotional response in your breath, body, or spirit as you consider your values? If so, how can you surrender this response and commit to God today?

NEW

Lectio Divina

I heard a loud voice from the throne say, "Look! God's dwelling is here with humankind. He will dwell with them, and they will be his peoples. God himself will be with them as their God. He will wipe away every tear from their eyes. Death will be no more. There will be no mourning, crying, or pain anymore, for the former things have passed away." Then the one seated on the throne said, "Look! I'm making all things new."

—Revelation 21:3-5, CEB

Pose

Cat-Cow

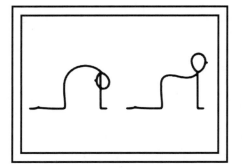

Counterpose

Downward-Facing Dog

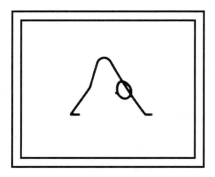

Breath Prayer

Inhale: God,
Exhale: make me new.

Aromatherapy

Basil

Reflect

How are you being made new by the Spirit? Scripture tells you that God dwells within you. Listen for and describe your response to that promise.

———

LIVE

Lectio Divina

Be imitators of God, as beloved children, and live in love, as Christ loved us and gave himself up for us, a fragrant offering and sacrifice to God.

—Ephesians 5:1-2

Pose	Counterpose
Bow	Child's Pose

Breath Prayer

Inhale: Sweet Jesus,
Exhale: I live because of you.

Aromatherapy

Spearmint

Reflect

Consider the fragrant offering of God's love for you. How do you live out love? In what ways are you living your life as an offering to God? In what ways does God invite you to love the life you have been given?

———

STRENGTH

Lectio Divina

Have you not known? Have you not heard?
The LORD is the everlasting God,
    the Creator of the ends of the earth.
He does not faint or grow weary;
    his understanding is unsearchable.
He gives power to the faint,
    and strengthens the powerless.

—Isaiah 40:28-29

Pose

Downward-Facing Dog

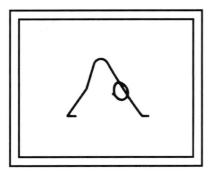

Counterpose

Mountain

Breath Prayer

Inhale: Everlasting God,
Exhale: renew my strength.

Aromatherapy

Tea Tree

Reflect

Where in your being (if anywhere) do you feel strong today? In body? In spirit? In mind? Where do you feel that you lack strength? How do you most need to be revived? Ask for God's strength in your life today.

————

FORGIVE

Lectio Divina

Jesus was praying in a certain place. When he finished, one of his disciples said, "Lord, teach us to pray, just as John taught his disciples." Jesus told them, "When you pray, say:
> 'Father, uphold the holiness of your name.
> Bring in your kingdom.
> Give us the bread we need for today.
> Forgive us our sins,
>   for we also forgive everyone who has wronged us.
> And don't lead us into temptation.'"

—Luke 11:1-4, CEB

Pose

Reclining Bound Angle

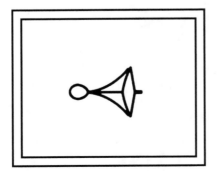

Counterpose

Knees-to-Chest

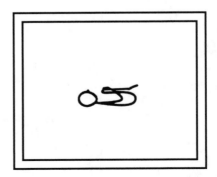

Breath Prayer

Inhale: Redeemer, forgive me.
Exhale: I forgive myself.

Aromatherapy

Thyme

Reflect

Where do you need forgiveness in your life? How may you offer forgiveness to others? to yourself? How could embracing forgiveness affect your breath, body, and spirit?

———

AMAZE

Lectio Divina

Peter said, "I have no silver or gold, but what I have I give you; in the name of Jesus Christ of Nazareth, stand up and walk." And he took him by the right hand and raised him up; and immediately his feet and ankles were made strong. Jumping up, he stood and began to walk, and he entered the temple with them, walking and leaping and praising God. All the people saw him walking and praising God, and they recognized him as the one who used to sit and ask for alms at the Beautiful Gate of the temple; and they were filled with wonder and amazement at what had happened to him.

—Acts 3:6-10

Pose

Mountain

Counterpose

Downward-Facing Dog

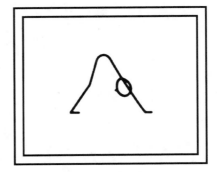

Breath Prayer

Inhale: Healer, open my eyes
Exhale: that I may see your wonders.

Aromatherapy

Cumin

Reflect

How has God amazed you in the past? What wonders have you seen or experienced? From what fears or insecurities do you long to be released? Ask God to amaze you today and release any physical, emotional, or spiritual barriers so that you may live authentically.

———

BOLD

Lectio Divina

"Be strong and bold; have no fear or dread of them, because it is the LORD your God who goes with you; he will not fail you or forsake you." Then Moses summoned Joshua and said to him in the sight of all Israel: "Be strong and bold, for you are the one who will go with this people into the land that the LORD has sworn to their ancestors to give them; and you will put them in possession of it. It is the LORD who goes before you. He will be with you; he will not fail you or forsake you. Do not fear or be dismayed."

—Deuteronomy 31:6-8

Pose

Warrior 1

Counterpose

Downward-Facing Dog

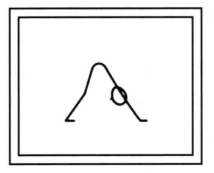

Breath Prayer

Inhale: Jesus, amidst it all,
Exhale: make me bold and courageous.

Aromatherapy

Fennel

Reflect

How does God's strength make you bold and courageous? When have you felt the need to be? How can you rely on God for boldness and courage today or in the future?

———

HEAL

Lectio Divina

Peace, peace, to the far and the near, says the LORD;
and I will heal them.

—Isaiah 57:19

Pose

Knees-to-Chest

Counterpose

Corpse

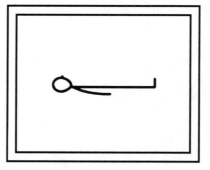

Breath Prayer

Inhale: Jehovah-Rapha,
Exhale: place your healing hands on me.

Aromatherapy

Allspice

Journal/Reflect

Where do you long for God's healing in your life? Where do you need God's healing touch on your physical body? What would God's healing look like in your life?

———

CELEBRATE

Lectio Divina

Let heaven celebrate!
    Let the earth rejoice!
    Let the nations say, "The LORD rules!"
Let the sea and everything in it roar!
    Let the countryside and everything in it celebrate!
Then the trees of the forest will shout out joyfully
    before the LORD, because he is coming
    to establish justice on earth!
Give thanks to the LORD because he is good,
    because his faithful love endures forever.

—1 Chronicles 16:31-34, CEB

Pose

Crescent Lunge

Counterpose

Downward-Facing Dog

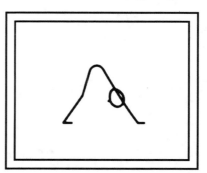

Breath Prayer

Inhale: Father,
Exhale: I celebrate your goodness.

Aromatherapy

Grapefruit

Reflect

What does it look like for you to shout and celebrate? Describe a time recently when you celebrated. How can you use your body to celebrate? How can you recognize and celebrate God's faithfulness in your life?

————

OPEN

Lectio Divina

Listen! I am standing at the door, knocking; if you hear my voice and open the door, I will come in to you and eat with you, and you with me. To the one who conquers I will give a place with me on my throne, just as I myself conquered and sat down with my Father on his throne.

—Revelation 3:20-21

Pose

Triangle

Counterpose

Standing Forward Bend

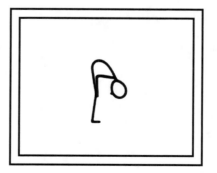

Breath Prayer

Inhale: Lord,
Exhale: open my eyes and ears to you.

Aromatherapy

Cypress

Reflect

How can you open yourself to God's activity? What parts of your breath, body, or spirit are open to God? What parts are not open to God? As you open your eyes and ears to God's activity in and around you, what do you expect to happen?

———

DREAM

Lectio Divina

Glory to God, who is able to do far beyond all that we could ask or imagine by his power at work within us; glory to him in the church and in Christ Jesus for all generations, forever and always. Amen.

Ephesians 3:20-21, CEB

Pose

Reclining Big Toe

Counterpose

Knees-to-Chest

Breath Prayer

Inhale: Abba,
Exhale: may your dreams be my dreams.

Aromatherapy

Clary Sage

Reflect

What are your dreams? Imagine God's dreams for you. What similarities do you notice between the two?

———

BELIEVE

Lectio Divina

"Blessed is she who believed that there would be a fulfillment of what was spoken to her by the Lord."

—Luke 1:45

Pose

Staff

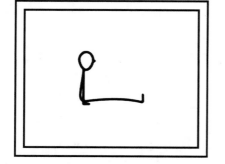

Counterpose

Seated Forward Bend

Breath Prayer

Inhale: Lord, I believe.
Exhale: Help my unbelief.

Aromatherapy

Frankincense

Reflect

Where do you see self-doubt in your life? God-doubt? In what areas of your life do you feel confident? What role has belief in God played in your past choices? How will your belief affect choices you make in the future?

———

PROTECT

Lectio Divina

"Every family of earth will be blessed because of you and your descendants. I am with you now, I will protect you everywhere you go, and I will bring you back to this land. I will not leave you until I have done everything that I have promised you."

—Genesis 28:14-15, CEB

Pose

Locust

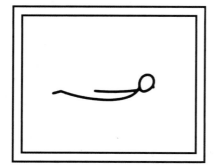

Counterpose

Child's Pose

Breath Prayer

Inhale: Yahweh,
Exhale: protect me on the path of life.

Aromatherapy

Birch

Reflect

Consider how God has protected you on your journey. Where will you need God's protection in the future? What decisions are you currently making in which you can ask for God's protection? What part of your being desires protection today?

———

RECEIVE

Lectio Divina

"Those who receive you are also receiving me, and those who receive me are receiving the one who sent me."

—Matthew 10:40, CEB

Pose

Chair

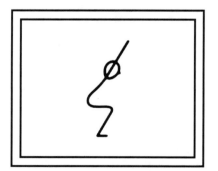

Counterpose

Standing Forward Bend

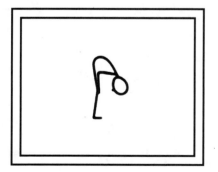

Breath Prayer

Inhale: Trinity God,
Exhale: allow me to fully receive you.

Aromatherapy

Sandalwood

Reflect

Recall a time when you received something you did not expect. How did you respond? Do you struggle to receive gifts from others? from God? What prevents you from fully receiving God?

———

ZEAL

Lectio Divina

A child is born to us, a son is given to us,
    and authority will be on his shoulders.
    He will be named Wonderful Counselor, Mighty God,
    Eternal Father, Prince of Peace.
There will be vast authority and endless peace
    for David's throne and for his kingdom,
    establishing and sustaining it
    with justice and righteousness
    now and forever.
The zeal of the LORD of heavenly forces will do this.

—Isaiah 9:6-7, CEB

Pose

Boat

Counterpose

Knees-to-Chest

Breath Prayer

Inhale: Wonderful Counselor,
Exhale: show me your goodness and zeal.

Aromatherapy

Cinnamon

Reflect

What makes your heart beat fast with excitement? What part of you longs for the goodness and zeal of the Lord? Where have you seen or experienced the zeal of the Lord in your own life?

———

THANKSGIVING

Lectio Divina

Do not worry about anything, but in everything by prayer and supplication with thanksgiving let your requests be made known to God. And the peace of God, which surpasses all understanding, will guard your hearts and your minds in Christ Jesus.

—Philippians 4:6-7

Pose

Pyramid

Counterpose

Mountain

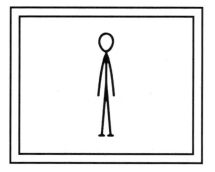

Breath Prayer

Inhale: Holy One,
Exhale: I come before you with thanks.

Aromatherapy

Orange

Reflect

What prayers will you bring before God today with gratitude and thanksgiving? Consider your own heart and mind. Do they feel guarded by God's peace? How can you offer gratitude for your body today?

———

DESIRE

Lectio Divina

May he grant you your heart's desire,
 and fulfill all your plans.
May we shout for joy over your victory,
 and in the name of our God set up our banners.
May the LORD fulfill all your petitions.

—Psalm 20:4-5

Pose

Camel

Counterpose

Standing Forward Bend

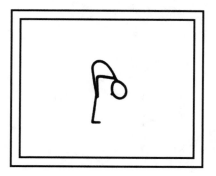

Breath Prayer

Inhale: Lord God,
Exhale: fulfill my heart's desires in your name.

Aromatherapy

Roman Chamomile

Reflect

What are the deepest desires of your heart? How can you share these desires with God? with others? What unexpected desires do you notice as you consider God's plans for you?

———

PREPARE

Lectio Divina

The beginning of the good news about Jesus Christ, God's Son, happened just as it was written about in the prophecy of Isaiah:

> Look, I am sending my messenger before you.
> He will prepare your way,
> a voice shouting in the wilderness:
> > "Prepare the way for the Lord;
> > make his paths straight."

—Mark 1:1-3, CEB

Pose

Bridge

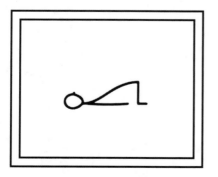

Counterpose

Knees-to-Chest

Breath Prayer

Inhale: Wise One,
Exhale: you prepare the way.

Aromatherapy

Patchouli

Reflect

Consider how God has prepared the way for you. How is God calling you to prepare for your life's journey? What preparation does your breath, body, and spirit need in this season of life?

———

UNIQUE

Lectio Divina

I give you a wise and discerning mind; no one like you has been before you and no one like you shall arise after you.

—1 Kings 3:12

Pose

Warrior 2

Counterpose

Downward-Facing Dog

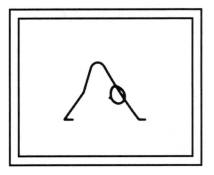

Breath Prayer

Inhale: Creator God,
Exhale: make me uniquely me.

Aromatherapy

Tangerine

Reflect

Ponder the traits, characteristics, or strengths that make you unique. How are you living as the unique person God created you to be? How do your imperfections draw you to the God who made you uniquely you?

———

CHANGE

Lectio Divina

God's name be praised
    from age to eternal age!
       Wisdom and might are his!
God is the one who changes times and eras,
    who dethrones one king, only to establish another,
       who grants wisdom to the wise and knowledge to those with insight.
                         —Daniel 2:20-21, CEB

Pose

Seated Forward Bend

Counterpose

Knees-to-Chest

Breath Prayer

Inhale: God, when seasons change,
Exhale: remind me of your wisdom.

Aromatherapy

Myrrh

Reflect

Reflect on how your body has offered you wisdom through changing seasons. When change occurs, how do you respond? How has change benefited you?

———

REJOICE

Lectio Divina

Rejoice always, pray without ceasing, give thanks in all circumstances; for this is the will of God in Christ Jesus for you.

—1 Thessalonians 5:16-18

Pose

Dancer

Counterpose

Standing Forward Bend

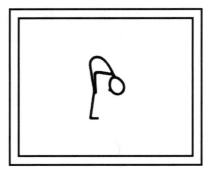

Breath Prayer

Inhale: God,
Exhale: show me how to rejoice.

Aromatherapy

Eucalyptus

Reflect

How do you rejoice in the good things of life? What does giving thanks in every situation look like? Describe a time in which you rejoiced in the midst of a difficult situation.

———

CLEANSE

Lectio Divina

Let's draw near with a genuine heart with the certainty that our faith gives us, since our hearts are sprinkled clean from an evil conscience and our bodies are washed with pure water.

—Hebrews 10:22, CEB

Pose

Reclining Spinal Twist

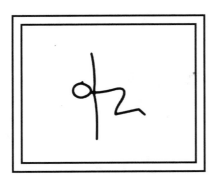

Counterpose

Knees-to-Chest

Breath Prayer

Inhale: Jesus, cleanse me
Exhale: and make me new.

Aromatherapy

Lemon

Reflect

Where are you in need of cleansing in your life? What has already been cleansed that you can fully release? How might it look for you to give thanks for and join God in the cleansing process of your life?

———

ENDURE

Lectio Divina

My brothers and sisters, think of the various tests you encounter as occasions for joy. After all, you know that the testing of your faith produces endurance. Let this endurance complete its work so that you may be fully mature, complete, and lacking in nothing.

—James 1:2-4, CEB

Pose

Downward-Facing Dog

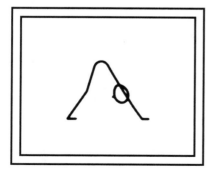

Counterpose

Child's Pose

Breath Prayer

Inhale: Endurance comes through you, Holy Spirit.
Exhale: I give thanks.

Aromatherapy

Ginger

Reflect

Recall a time in your life when you needed endurance. How are you able to endure life's challenges—through your body or spirit? In what parts of your life do you need God's strength and endurance?

———

FUTURE

Lectio Divina

My child, eat honey, for it is good,
    and the drippings of the honeycomb are sweet to your taste.
Know that wisdom is such to your soul;
    if you find it, you will find a future,
    and your hope will not be cut off.

—Proverbs 24:13-14

Pose

Extended Side Angle

Counterpose

Mountain

Breath Prayer

Inhale: O Lord,
Exhale: give me hope for the future.

Aromatherapy

Peppermint

Reflect

If wisdom is like honey to your soul, how do you embrace it as a gift for your future? For what do you hope? How can you open yourself both physically and spiritually to God's hope for your future?

———

ASK

Lectio Divina

"Now, my daughter, do not be afraid. I will do for you all that you ask, for all the assembly of my people know that you are a worthy woman."

—Ruth 3:11

Pose

Simple Sitting

Counterpose

Staff

Breath Prayer

Inhale: I am not afraid, Lord.
Exhale: I ask for what I need from you today.

Aromatherapy

Ylang-Ylang

Reflect

As you ask God for what you need today, what part of you (if any) is afraid? What part of your body most identifies with experiencing fear? Consider placing your hands on that part of your body and asking God for what you need today.

———

LOVE

Lectio Divina

Love is patient; love is kind; love is not envious or boastful or arrogant or rude. It does not insist on its own way; it is not irritable or resentful; it does not rejoice in wrongdoing, but rejoices in the truth. It bears all things, believes all things, hopes all things, endures all things.

—1 Corinthians 13:4-7

Pose

Cobra

Counterpose

Child's Pose

Breath Prayer

Inhale: Loving God,
Exhale: teach me to love.

Aromatherapy

Rose

Reflect

Is the gift of love required for other spiritual gifts to be effective? Why or why not? How do you express love for yourself? How do you express love for others?

———

EXALT

Lectio Divina

Where can we find the strength to praise him?
    For he is greater than all his works.
Awesome is the Lord and very great,
    and marvelous is his power.
Glorify the Lord and exalt him as much as you can,
    for he surpasses even that.
When you exalt him, summon all your strength,
    and do not grow weary, for you cannot praise him enough.
                    —Sirach* 43:28-30

Pose

Warrior 3

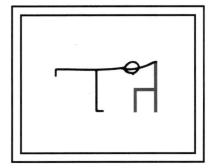

Counterpose

Mountain

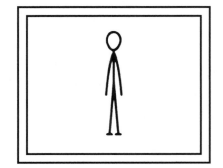

90

Breath Prayer

Inhale: Strong Jehovah,
Exhale: I exalt you.

Aromatherapy

Clove Bud

Reflect

In what ways do you exalt God with your breath, body, and spirit? What parts of you do you consider strong and courageous? How has God made you strong?

———

*Sirach is found in the Apocrypha/Deuterocanonical scriptures and is considered a wisdom book.

PRUNE

Lectio Divina

"I am the true vine, and my Father is the vineyard keeper. He removes any of my branches that don't produce fruit, and he trims any branch that produces fruit so that it will produce even more fruit. You are already trimmed because of the word I have spoken to you."

—John 15:1-3, CEB

Pose

Eagle

Counterpose

Mountain

Breath Prayer

Inhale: Heavenly Father,
Exhale: prune me so I may grow.

Aromatherapy

Rosemary

Reflect

What fruit do you produce thanks to God? How do you remain focused on God during seasons of pruning? What aspects of your life need to be pruned so that God may grow you?

———

REST

Lectio Divina

It is in vain that you rise up early
　　and go late to rest,
eating the bread of anxious toil;
　　for he gives sleep to his beloved.

—Psalm 127:2

Pose

Open Angle

Counterpose

Knees-to-Chest

Breath Prayer

Inhale: God of heaven,
Exhale: allow me to rest in you.

Aromatherapy

Vetiver

Reflect

When and how do you embrace rest in your life? How do you practice resting intentionally? In what ways does resting your body and mind allow you
to feel grounded and refreshed?

———

JOY

Lectio Divina

I will rejoice in the Lord.

    I will rejoice in the God of my deliverance.

The Lord God is my strength.

    He will set my feet like the deer.

    He will let me walk upon the heights.

—Habakkuk 3:18-19, CEB

Pose

Half-Moon

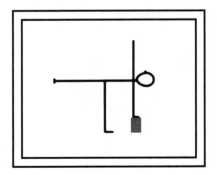

Counterpose

Standing Forward Bend

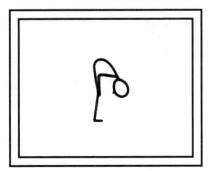

Breath Prayer

Inhale: In you, Lord,
Exhale: I find joy.

Aromatherapy

Lemongrass

Reflect

How will you engage your breath, body, and spirit today in a way that brings joy? How will you seek joy when your feet do not feel steady? Your sense of smell has the remarkable ability of connecting you to memories. What scents remind you of joyful memories?

———————

MOURN

Lectio Divina

Jesus began to weep.

—John 11:35

Pose

Bridge

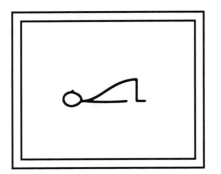

Counterpose

Corpse

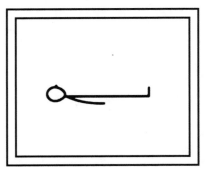

Breath Prayer

Inhale: O Holy One,
Exhale: comfort my heart.

Aromatherapy

Geranium

Reflect

What makes you weep? Over what parts of your life are you mourning or grieving? How can you invite your entire self into that process? How does God protect you as you mourn?

———

TRUST

Lectio Divina

"The LORD will fight for you. You just keep still."

—Exodus 14:14, CEB

Pose

Inclined Plane

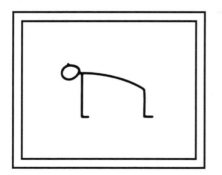

Counterpose

Seated Forward Bend

Breath Prayer

Inhale: In the stillness, Lord,
Exhale: I trust you with all my strength.

Aromatherapy

Marjoram

Reflect

How does your trust grow in the waiting seasons? What areas of your life are lacking trust? Recall a time you had no choice but to be still and trust God. What did you learn?

———

FREEDOM

Lectio Divina

Now that you have been set free from sin and become slaves to God, you have the consequence of a holy life, and the outcome is eternal life.

—Romans 6:22, CEB

Pose

Wide-Legged Forward Bend

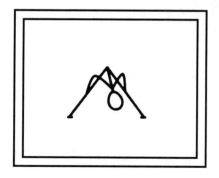

Counterpose

Mountain

Breath Prayer

Inhale: Yahweh,
Exhale: you bring freedom.

Aromatherapy

Bergamot

Reflect

Do you feel free? If so, how can you celebrate this freedom you have been given? If not, how can you begin to embrace freedom with your whole self?

————

HOPE

Lectio Divina

I pray that the eyes of your heart will have enough light to see what is the hope of God's call, what is the richness of God's glorious inheritance among believers, and what is the overwhelming greatness of God's power that is working among us believers. This power is conferred by the energy of God's powerful strength.

—Ephesians 1:18-19, CEB

Pose

Happy Baby

Counterpose

Bridge

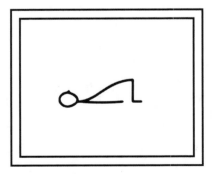

Breath Prayer

Inhale: Mighty God,
Exhale: give me hope in you.

Aromatherapy

Coriander

Reflect

What are God's hopes for your life? What are your hopes? How does God offer hope to others through you? How can your path of healing and wholeness offer hope to the world?

———

WISDOM

Lectio Divina

Let the word of Christ dwell in you richly; teach and admonish one another in all wisdom; and with gratitude in your hearts sing psalms, hymns, and spiritual songs to God.

—Colossians 3:16

Pose

Fish

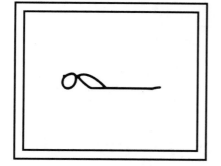

Counterpose

Knees-to-Chest

Breath Prayer

Inhale: Christ of all,
Exhale: fill me with your wisdom.

Aromatherapy

Black Pepper

Reflect

How does God's wisdom shape you? In what ways do you clothe yourself with the wisdom of God? How does your body invite you to listen for the wisdom of God?

———

SECURE

Lectio Divina

"If you direct your heart rightly,
    you will stretch out your hands toward him.
If iniquity is in your hand, put it far away,
    and do not let wickedness reside in your tents.
Surely then you will lift up your face without blemish;
    you will be secure, and will not fear."

—Job 11:13-15

Pose

Tree

Counterpose

Mountain

Breath Prayer

Inhale: When I look to you, God,
Exhale: I am secure.

Aromatherapy

Jasmine

Reflect

What parts of your life long to be grounded in God? When you consider the emotion of fear, how does your physical body respond? How can changing your posture affect your sense of security?

———

COMMUNE

Lectio Divina

Conduct yourselves with all humility, gentleness, and patience. Accept each other with love, and make an effort to preserve the unity of the Spirit with the peace that ties you together. You are one body and one spirit, just as God also called you in one hope. There is one Lord, one faith, one baptism, and one God and Father of all, who is over all, through all, and in all.

—Ephesians 4:2-6, CEB

Pose

Sphinx

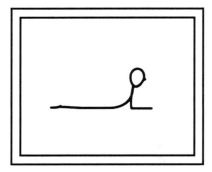

Counterpose

Child's Pose

Breath Prayer

Inhale: Abba, draw me nearer.
Exhale: Draw me nearer to thee.

Aromatherapy

Cedar

Reflect

How is your breath, body, and spirit one with God? In what ways do you use your body to draw nearer to God? How does drawing nearer to God allow you to commune with others?

———

PEACE

Lectio Divina

May the Lord of peace himself give you peace at all times in all ways. The Lord be with all of you.

—2 Thessalonians 3:16

Pose

Hero

Counterpose

Downward-Facing Dog

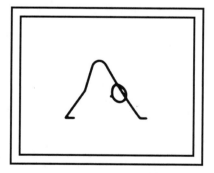

Breath Prayer

Inhale: Prince of Peace,
Exhale: fill my presence with your presence.

Aromatherapy

Lavender

Reflect

How do you receive and experience God's peace? How can you share that peace with others? Does the journey of listening for God with your whole self assist you in receiving the gift of God's peace?

———

REFLECTION QUESTIONS
AFTER COMPLETION

I hope this book served as an invitation to self-awareness, health, and wholeness through holy listening. Continue to honor your body as you listen for God's movement in your life. Be kind to yourself as you slow down to embrace new ways of listening. The Holy Spirit is with you. May the gift of your breath, body, and spirit continue to draw you nearer to your Creator and give you peace on your healing journey. If you kept a written journal during this process, revisit your own words and consider the following questions:

- Where and how did you depart from the crowds and discover sacred space during this journey?
- What themes stood out or spoke most clearly to you? What patterns do you notice in your responses?
- What did you learn about yourself? Where did you struggle? Where did you find delight?
- What unhealed wounds will require a counselor, therapist, pastor, or spiritual director to accompany you on your journey?
- What new discoveries did you make about your breath, body, and spirit? How did awareness in your body and breath shift or deepen your listening during these forty days?
- How did this time awaken your senses in other areas of your life? How did it provide care for your soul?
- What resistance did you face?
- Which ancient tools most engaged your listening time with God? Which will you take with you past these forty days?
- How has your own spiritual formation journey shaped others in your home, community, and world?

A CLOSING BLESSING

I bow my knees before the Father, from whom every family in heaven and on earth takes its name. I pray that, according to the riches of his glory, he may grant that you may be strengthened in your inner being with power through his Spirit, and that Christ may dwell in your hearts through faith, as you are being rooted and grounded in love. I pray that you may have the power to comprehend, with all the saints, what is the breadth and length and height and depth, and to know the love of Christ that surpasses knowledge, so that you may be filled with all the fullness of God. Now to him who by the power at work within us is able to accomplish abundantly far more than all we can ask or imagine, to him be glory in the church and in Christ Jesus to all generations, forever and ever. Amen.

—Ephesians 3:14-21

Through exploring a life with God, you have embraced the wisdom of your breath, body, and spirit. I hope this journey of holy listening is simply beginning for you. As you humbly discover the wisdom and gifts bestowed upon you, I pray you continue to seek the closeness of your Creator. May God bless you and others as you continue to listen with your breath, body, and spirit. May you continue making space for God's presence as you discern God's activity in your life. May you deepen your appreciation of God and of yourself through new habits and growing knowledge. May you be open to God's guidance as you continue being shaped into the person God created you to be.

APPENDIX

Warm-up Sequence

Warming-up your body is an important step to complete prior to trying the suggested yoga postures. A warm-up limbers the body, preparing you physically for practice. It also allows you to focus your heart and mind. There are a variety of warm-up sequences so feel free to use one you already practice or try the seated warm-up below. For this sequence, you may want to place a folded blanket or pillow under your hips to help find length in your spine.

Simple Sitting

Sit on a blanket or pillow with your legs crossed and knees wide. Draw your navel toward your spine, and stretch the crown of your head toward the ceiling.

One Hand at Heart

Bring your right hand to your heart and your left hand to your belly. Fully inhale and exhale through your nose. Notice the rhythm of your heart and breath.

Lower and Lift Chin

With your hands on your thighs, continue to stretch the crown of your head toward the ceiling. Slowly lower your chin to your chest for a breath, then slowly lift your chin for a breath. Move between lifting and lowering the chin before returning to a neutral position.

Seated Twist

From Simple Sitting, place your right hand on the ground and your left hand on the outside of your right leg. Lengthen your spine, and turn to look over your right shoulder. Repeat for the opposite side of your body.

Seated Forward Bend

Sit with your legs in front of you, knees slightly bent. Roll your hips forward as you keep your back long, sliding your hands down your legs as you move your heart toward your toes.

Hands at Lower Back

From Simple Sitting, switch how your legs are crossed. Bring your hands to your lower back, draw the elbows toward each other, and open your chest. Lift your gaze if you feel comfortable doing so.

Seated Side Bend

From Simple Sitting, lower your left hand to the ground. Reach up and over with your right arm, bringing it by your ear. Repeat for the opposite side of your body.

Simple Sitting

Return to Simple Sitting, and check in with your body. You may wish to remain in this position to explore the *lectio divina*, breath prayer, or aromatherapy prompts prior to moving through the theme's pose and counterpose.

Chair Modifications

For some reading this book, physical movement is not feasible or is limited due to short-term injury, chronic pain, disability, or a variety of other reasons. I recognize and honor the physical limitations of your body and encourage you to consider honoring them while on this journey. I don't say this to discount your physical struggles but instead to invite God's Spirit to work through your inner and outer wounds.

Consider using Seated Mountain for Chair (explained below) throughout the book, or explore chair modifications for certain postures. A chair will support your body in the postures, allowing you to feel grounded and steady. The following modified postures represent only a small sampling of how poses can be modified with a chair for accessibility. Choose a sturdy chair for these exercises (preferably a chair without arms, although some of these postures may be accessible from a wheelchair). Remember that pain is a warning that signals you to adjust or select another posture.

Seated Mountain for Chair

Sit upright on the edge of a chair with your feet parallel. Root the four corners of your feet into the ground. Draw your navel toward your back, and allow your hands to rest on your thighs. Expand your chest as you draw your shoulder blades toward the back of the body to open your heart space. Sit tall as you lift the crown of your head toward the ceiling. Rather than leaning back, leave space between your back and the chair. You may also consider placing a block or pillow between your lower back and the chair.

Camel for Chair

From Seated Mountain, place your hands on your lower back. Draw your elbows toward each other and open your chest. Lift your gaze if you feel comfortable doing so.

Cat-Cow for Chair

From Seated Mountain, exhale as you draw your belly in and round your back like a cat. Inhale and roll your hips forward, arching your back and expanding your chest. Move slowly between cat and cow ten times.

Side Bend for Chair

From Seated Mountain, ground both legs as you lower your left hand to the seat or the leg of your chair. Reach up and over with your right arm, bringing it by your ear. Repeat for the opposite side of your body.

Simple Seated Twist for Chair

From Seated Mountain, bring your hands to the outside of your right thigh. Lengthen your spine, and slowly turn to look over your right shoulder. Slowly return to Seated Mountain. Repeat for the opposite side of your body.

Warrior I for Chair

From Seated Mountain, bring your right leg to the right side of the chair, straddling the chair and extending your back leg. Bend your right knee to a 90-degree angle, extend your arms overhead, and relax your shoulders away from your ears. Repeat for the opposite side of your body.

Warrior 2 for Chair

From Seated Mountain, bring your right leg to the right side of the chair, straddling the chair and extending through your back leg. Turn your hips to the front of the chair, bend your right knee to a 90-degree angle, extend your arms long, and bring your shoulders away from your ears. Repeat for the opposite side of your body.

Relaxation for Chair

Sit upright in your chair, allowing your back to touch the chair. Place a pillow or block behind your back if desired. Allow your feet to rest naturally on the floor or on the seat of another chair in front of you.

Posture Index

Always warm up your body with gentle stretching before exploring the poses. (See pages 116–17.) Breathing in and out through the nose, hold each posture for five, ten, fifteen, or twenty breaths before moving to the next pose. (Note: The length of time you hold postures may increase as your yoga practice evolves.) As time allows, I encourage you to close your practice with relaxation. (See page 128.) As noted earlier, no props are required to practice these poses, but you may want to have a sturdy chair available for balancing postures. For safety and comfort, use a nonslip yoga mat and remove socks prior to practicing standing postures. The posture instructions below are modified to be safe for beginners. The Sanskrit name of each posture is noted in parentheses.

Boat (Paripurna Navasana)

From a seated position, bend your knees toward your chest. Allow your feet to remain on the floor for added support or lift one foot off the ground at a time as you lengthen your spine. Draw your inner thighs together, and balance on your sitting bones. Hold the backs of your thighs, or reach forward with your arms.

Bow (Dhanurasana)

Beginning on your belly, bend your knees as you reach back toward your feet to grasp your ankles. Lift your heart as you reach your arms back, or you may press your feet into your hands and lift your heels toward the ceiling.

Bridge (Setu Bandha Sarvangasana)

Lie on your back, and bend your knees so that the soles of the feet are flat on the ground and parallel, with your ankles stacked under your knees. Slowly lift your hips toward the ceiling while squeezing your shoulder blades closer together and slightly lifting your chin to protect your neck. You may consider clasping your hands beneath your lower back. Place a block under your hips for additional support.

Camel (Ustrasana)

Kneeling on the floor, stack your shoulders, hips, and knees. Lift the crown of your head, lengthening your spine. Place your hands on your lower back with your fingertips facing either down or up. Engage your legs while pressing the tops of your feet into the floor. Draw your elbows toward each other and open your chest. Lift your gaze if you feel comfortable doing so.

Cat-Cow (Marjaryasana-Bitilasana)

Begin on your hands and knees with your wrists underneath your shoulders and your knees underneath your hips. Engage your core, exhaling as you draw your belly in and round your back. Inhale and soften your belly, filling your lungs as you lift the crown of your head, open your heart, and arch your back. Repeat ten times.

Chair (Utkatasana)

Stand tall. Slowly bend your knees as you sink your hips back and down as if you were going to sit in a chair. Lift your arms in front or overhead beside your ears. Draw your navel toward your spine, lengthening your lower back. Soften and release your shoulders away from your ears.

Child's Pose (Balasana)

Begin on your hands and knees with your big toes touching. Sink your hips back toward your heels, and walk your hands forward. Rest your torso on your thighs.

Cobra (Bhujangasana)

Begin on your belly. Bend your elbows and place your hands on the  floor near your ribs. Engage your core, and slowly lift your heart as you press your pelvis and the tops of your feet into the floor.

Corpse (Savasana)

Lie flat on your back. Relax your feet and legs, allowing your arms to rest beside you with palms facing up. Soften your body completely from head to toe.

Crescent Lunge (Alanasana)

Stand tall. Step your left foot back into a lunge. Bend your right knee, stacking your knee over your ankle. Lift your arms overhead, and draw your shoulders down and away from your ears. Or you may choose to bring your hands to heart center. Repeat for the opposite side of your body.

Dancer (Natarajasana)

Stand tall with your right hand on a wall. Bend your left knee, holding on to your foot with your hand or a strap. Press your foot into the hand or strap while lifting your heart. Repeat for the opposite side of your body.

Downward-Facing Dog (Adho Mukha Svanasana)

Begin on your hands and knees. Tuck your toes, and lift your hips toward the ceiling. With hands flat on the ground, press your knuckles into the ground. Lift your shoulders toward your hips. Engage your legs, softening or bending your knees as needed.

Eagle (Garudasana)

Stand tall. Lift your left leg and cross it over your right leg at the knee (or keep both feet on the ground). Lower your hips back and down. Cross your right elbow over your left, and give yourself a hug or wrap your arms. Repeat for the opposite side of your body.

Extended Side Angle (Utthita Parsvakonasana)

Stand tall, and open your legs about four feet apart. Turn your right foot out 90 degrees, and bend your right knee, stacking it over your ankle. Allow your right hand or forearm to rest on your right thigh. Reach your left arm toward the ceiling as you open your chest. Repeat for the opposite side of your body.

Fish (Matsyasana)

Begin on your back with your arms by your side. Lift your heart and arch your back while squeezing your shoulder blades together. Keep your head safely on the ground.

Gate (Parighasana)

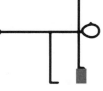

Kneel on the floor, and stretch your right leg out to the side. Reach your left hand toward the ceiling, engaging your core as you slide your right hand down your leg as far as feels comfortable. Repeat for the opposite side of your body.

Half-Moon (Ardha Chandrasana)

Stand tall. Open your legs about four feet apart, turning your right foot out 90 degrees. While bending your knee, place your right hand about twelve inches in front of your right foot on a chair or block. Lift your left leg as you straighten your right leg, reaching your heart and left hand toward the ceiling. Repeat for the opposite side of your body.

Happy Baby (Ananda Balasana)

Lie on your back, and draw your knees to your chest. Hold on to the back of your knees or the soles of your feet. Press your head, shoulders, and tailbone into the ground while aligning your spine.

Hero (Virasana)

Kneeling on the floor, sit on your heels or on a block. Draw your navel toward your spine. Lift the crown of your head toward the ceiling, and rest your hands on your thighs.

Inclined Plane (Purvottanasana)

Sit on the floor, pressing your hands and feet into the floor as you lift your hips toward the ceiling.

Knees-to-Chest (Apanasana)

Lie on your back, and hug your knees to your chest. Press your head, shoulders, and tailbone into the floor. Notice how a slight tuck of your chin elongates your spine.

Legs-up-the-Wall (Viparita Karani)

Lie on the ground with your feet up the wall. Turn your palms toward the ceiling.

Locust (Salabhasana)

Lie on your belly with arms and hands by your side, palms down. Engage your core as you slowly lift your heart and legs.

Mountain (Tadasana)

Stand tall with your feet parallel, rooting the four corners of your feet into the ground. Engage your legs and core while lifting the crown of your head toward the ceiling. Allow your arms to open as you expand your chest. Draw your shoulder blades together to open your heart space.

Open-Angle (Upavistha Konasana)

Begin seated with your legs open and your toes pointed toward the ceiling. Press your hands into the ground beside you, elongating your spine as you lift your chest.

Pyramid (Parsvottanasana)

Stand tall. Step back with your left foot. Hinging at your hips, slide your hands down your right leg. Repeat for the opposite side of your body.

Reclining Big Toe (Supta Padangusthasana)

Begin by lying on your back. Pull your right knee in toward your chest, and press your heel toward the ceiling while holding the back of your right leg. Press your shoulders and tailbone into the ground.

Reclining Bound Angle (Supta Baddha Konasana)

Begin on your back with your knees bent. Slowly lower your knees to the floor, and bring the soles of your feet together. Allow your arms to rest by your side. Place a pillow or block under each thigh for support.

Reclining Spinal Twist (Jathara Parivartanasana)

Lie on your back as you bring your knees toward your chest. Open your arms perpendicular to your body. Engage your core, and slowly lower your knees to the right as you roll your head to the left. Repeat for the opposite side of your body.

Seated Forward Bend (Paschimottanasana)

Sit with your legs in front of you and your knees slightly bent. Roll your hips forward and keep your back long as you slide your hands down your legs and move your heart toward your toes.

Simple Sitting (Sukhasana)

Sit on a blanket or pillow with your legs crossed and knees wide. Draw your navel toward your spine, and stretch the crown of your head toward the ceiling.

Sphinx (Salamba Bhujangasana)

Begin on your belly, and prop yourself up on your elbows. Engage your core, and slowly lift your heart. Press your pelvis and the tops of your feet into the floor. Draw your shoulders back and down toward your hips.

Staff (Dandasana)

Sit with your knees bent or legs straight. Flex your toes toward your face as you press your thighs and hands into the floor. Roll your shoulder blades back and down toward your hips. Lift the crown of your head toward the ceiling.

Standing Forward Bend (Uttanasana)

Stand tall with your feet parallel. With a slight bend in your knees, roll your hips forward, sliding your hands down your legs. Relax your neck, and let your head hang heavy.

Tree (Vrksasana)

Stand tall. Lift the sole of your left foot to your right ankle, calf, or thigh. Keep hands at heart center, or slowly lift arms overhead. Roll your shoulders back and down. Allow your gaze to softly rest on a point in the horizon. Repeat for the opposite side of your body.

Triangle (Utthita Trikonasana)

Stand tall. Open your legs about four feet apart, and turn your right foot out 90 degrees. Bend your hips to the right as you slide your right hand down your thigh. Raise your left arm, spinning your heart to the left. Repeat for the opposite side of your body.

Warrior 1 (Virabhadrasana I)

Stand tall. Step back with your left foot, allowing your hips to remain forward. Bend your right knee, stacking your knee and ankle. Keep your hands at heart center or extend your arms overhead. Roll your shoulders back and down toward your hips, and draw your navel toward your spine. Repeat for the opposite side of your body.

Warrior 2 (Virabhadrasana II)

Stand tall. Open your legs about four feet apart. Turn your right foot out 90 degrees, and bend your right knee, stacking it over your ankle. Open your arms wide and look at your right hand. Repeat for the opposite side of your body.

Warrior 3 (Virabhadrasana III)

Stand tall. Roll your hips forward as you place your hands on the back of a chair. Lift your left leg, squaring your hips with the chair and drawing your navel toward your spine. Repeat for the opposite side of your body.

Wide-Legged Forward Bend (Prasarita Padottanasana)

Stand tall. Open your legs about four feet apart. Soften your knees, and place your hands on your hips. Roll your hips forward as you slide your hands down your legs, pressing evenly through your feet.

Relaxation

A time of relaxation concludes yoga practice. While many relaxation postures exist, the Corpse pose (Savasana) most commonly closes a yoga practice. Corpse is included in some of the postures throughout this devotional. If time allows, consider following the pose and counterpose with an extended time (five to fifteen minutes) in Corpse pose. Many teachers consider this final resting pose to be the most important part of a yoga practice. In fact, if it were the only posture you practiced, you would still be practicing yoga. In addition to releasing any tension in the body while practicing Corpse pose, consider releasing your thoughts, worries, and stresses as well. Allow your breath to remain steady, and rest in God's presence. You may also modify the pose in a chair (see page 119) or by rolling a blanket and placing it under your knees.

What's in a Theme?

This book was created based on my own experience of using my body to listen for God's activity. *Lectio divina*, yoga, breath prayer, aromatherapy, and journaling have been essential components of my journey. You may be curious how each theme was compiled or why certain oils or postures were selected for a certain theme or Bible passage. Through research of each theme, I selected specific yoga postures and essential oils based on their emotional or physical properties. For example, rose essential oil is referred to as the oil of love, and, for that reason, I included it with the theme *Love*.[1] That theme includes the yoga pose Cobra (Bhujangasana)—a chest-opening stretch. Heart and chest openers expand your chest and rib cage, offering more physical space. After a heart-opening posture, you may find that you are more open—both physically and emotionally—to offering and receiving love. I chose each posture and oil for the daily themes after research, practice, and exploration. That being said, the prompts are merely suggestions. Ultimately, your body offers the wisdom to embrace the scripture passages, yoga postures, prayers, scents, or questions for which it most longs. Allow this book to serve as a guide, but trust your inner wisdom along the way.

SUGGESTIONS FOR SMALL GROUPS

The themes in this book are designed for individual reflection but may also be used in a small-group experience. Used as daily themes, a group could explore forty days of listening together during Lent or any other time of year. Used as weekly themes, this guide offers prompts for nearly a year of reflection. Individual themes can also be used in a small-group workshop, a weekend retreat, or a Christian yoga class.

A small group may have one leader, or members of the group may take turns. If you are choosing a leader for your small group, consider asking someone with small-group leadership experience. This person should honor participants' time and respect different healing journeys.

Tips for Small-Group Leaders

- Create a sacred space for your small group. Light a candle, incorporate religious symbols or art. Consider using a sound machine or playing soft music if you are meeting in a space where distractions are prevalent.
- Honor participants in breath, body, and spirit, recognizing differences in their relationships with God and their bodies.
- Open and close each group discussion in silence, focusing on the gift of breath.
- Allow space for participants to share their experiences on the spiritual journey and the ways God interacts with them.
- Refrain from offering your own opinion, cross talking, problem-solving, or fixing. Simply listen to the participants, and be present.
- Practice *lectio divina* as a group, or invite participants to share what they heard after practicing this reading style individually.
- Consider inviting a certified yoga instructor to lead the group in a yoga session or a trained spiritual director to facilitate group spiritual direction as you listen for and discern God's activity together.

- Set aside time to journal together at the end of the session. Ask participants to reflect on what they have experienced individually and as a group.
- Explore aromatherapy together. Use an oil diffuser during your small-group sessions, or invite participants to bring their own essential oils. A little oil goes a long way, and sharing with friends is a great way to experience the benefits of a variety of essential oils.
- Spend time together in community outside of your small-group session. Eat, pray, move, and/or create with your small group.

For more information on the various tools mentioned in this book or for additional ways to use this book in your small group, visit www.ExploringPeace.com.

NOTES

Introduction

1. Bessel A. van der Kolk, M.D., *The Body Keeps the Score: Brain, Mind, and Body in the Healing of Trauma* (New York: Penguin Books, 2014), 1–4.
2. Flora Slosson Wuellner, *Prayer and Our Bodies* (Nashville, TN: Upper Room Books, 1987), 10.
3. M. Robert Mulholland Jr., *Shaped by the Word: The Power of Scripture in Spiritual Formation, rev. ed.* (Nashville, TN: Upper Room Books, 2000), 25.
4. Wuellner, *Prayer and Our Bodies*, 9.

Holy Listening

1. Henri J. M. Nouwen, Michael J. Christensen, and Rebecca Laird, *Spiritual Direction: Wisdom for the Long Walk of Faith* (San Francisco: HarperOne, 2006), 22.
2. Margaret Guenther, *Holy Listening: The Art of Spiritual Direction* (Lanham, MD: Cowley Publications, 1992), 85.

The Ancient Tools

1. Jan Johnson, *Savoring God's Word: Cultivating the Soul-transforming Practice of Scripture Meditation* (Colorado Springs, CO: NavPress, 2004), 42.
2. Ibid.
3. Brooke Boon, *Holy Yoga: Exercise for the Christian Body and Soul* (New York: FaithWords, 2007), 16.
4. Adele Ahlberg Calhoun, *Spiritual Disciplines Handbook: Practices That Transform Us* (Downers Grove, IL: InterVarsity Press, 2005), 204–7.
5. Elizabeth Anne Jones, *Awaken to Healing Fragrance: The Power of Essential Oil Therapy* (Berkeley, CA: North Atlantic Books, 2010), 230.

6. Sheppard B. Kominars, *Write for Life: Healing Body, Mind, & Spirit through Journal Writing* (Cleveland, OH: Cleveland Clinic Press, 2007). Kindle edition.

7. Nouwen. *Spiritual Direction*, xv.

The Invitation

1. Wuellner, *Prayer and Our Bodies*, 59.

What's in a Theme?

1. Valerie Ann Worwood, *Aromatherapy for the Soul: Healing the Spirit with Fragrance and Essential Oils* (Novato, CA: New World Library, 2006), 273.

ABOUT THE AUTHOR

After a life-changing health crisis, Whitney R. Simpson embraced a journey toward healing and wholeness, using her breath, body, and spirit. Her new lifestyle included time on a yoga mat and regular sessions with a spiritual director, which set the foundation for her path to recovery. Whitney later pursued professional certification in spiritual formation from Garrett-Evangelical Theological Seminary. She now serves as a retreat facilitator, spiritual director, and yoga instructor. As a survivor of stroke, brain surgery, and cancer—all before the age of thirty-one—she seeks to experience and share the gifts of God's peace no matter the circumstances. Connect with Whitney at www.ExploringPeace.com.